The Little Piano Girl

By Ann Ingalls & Maryann Macdonald
Illustrated by Giselle Potter

Houghton Mifflin Books for Children
HOUGHTON MIFFLIN HARCOURT
BOSTON   NEW YORK   2010

Chug-ga
Chug-ga

CLappety
CLaP
CLaP

The night she left Georgia, Mary couldn't see anything
but lights out the train window ... but she could hear!
She listened to the train and clapped out its sound on her knees.
She sang the sound of its whistle.
"Chug-ga, chug-ga, chug-ga ... Toot! Toot!"
The train went faster, leaving home behind:
"Clackety-clack! Clackety-clack! Clackety-clack!"
Mary clapped and sang softly, so that Mama
and her sister, Mamie, could sleep.

By the time they arrived at the big station in Pittsburgh the next morning, Mary had sung herself to sleep, too.

More than anything else, Mary loved music. Back in Atlanta, her mama had played the organ for their church. Sometimes she played at home, too. When Mary was three, Mama played a tune, holding Mary on her lap.

Sweet Home

As the last notes sounded through the room, Mary reached out and played them back to her mother. Mama stood up and Mary went tumbling. Mama cried to her neighbors,
"Come hear this! Come hear my baby girl play!"

After that, Mary was always at the keyboard. When she pounded
the keys, she made thunder. When she tapped them, it rained.
Sounds rose up from her playing, soft like the sun beaming,
sharp like frogs calling, lonely like train whistles in the night . . .
all from a place safe and secret inside her.

But when the family moved from Atlanta to Pittsburgh, the organ stayed behind.

"It's just too big and heavy," Mama said. "We'll have to sell it."

They took their Victrola with the megaphone so Mary could listen to music, but without her organ, how could she play?

The Smoky City ... that's what people called Pittsburgh.
A war was going on
and the nation needed steel for ships and guns.
There were jobs in the Pittsburgh steel mills.
Their smokestacks poured fumes into the sky,
high above the Monongahela River
and the Allegheny Mountains
and all the wooden houses tucked in
around them.

Aunt Hattie and Uncle Joe Epster lived in one of those houses. They welcomed Mary and her mother and sister. But the neighbors didn't want any newcomers, and someone threw bricks though the Epsters' windows.

Others called the family mean names. The neighbor girl with the long curls shut the door in Mary's face. "My mother says not to play with you," she said.

Seven-year-old Mary didn't have shoes for her first day at Lincoln School, so she borrowed her mother's. Mama had dainty feet, size two. Mary's heels stuck out of the back of her mother's shoes. A big, scary girl pulled her hair.

"Where'd you get those funny shoes?"

Ugly names and cruel words …
Mary called them "bad sounds,"
and she taught herself to play them out.
Even without a keyboard, she could do it.
Tapping on the tabletop, she beat back the bad sounds
and sang out her sadness.
She crooned and whispered and shouted out
until her spirit was lifted free.

No one remembers exactly how it all started,
how Mary began playing piano again.
One story goes like this:
She was picking dandelions one day. Lucille,
a lady everyone knew from church, walked by.
   "Say, why aren't you off with your friends?"
Lucille asked. Mary just shook her head, and
couldn't say. Lucille shifted the bag on her hip.
   "I've got some ice cream in this bag," she said.
   "If you don't come
   and help me
   eat it, it'll melt."

Mary's big brown eyes grew wide.

"Yes, ma'am," she said.

She sat down at the table in Lucille's house. A lace tablecloth covered it, and the dishes all matched. Best of all, a shiny piano stood in the corner of the room. Mary's shy eyes stole glances at it.

"You play the piano any?" Lucille asked.

Mary nodded.

"Okay, girl," said Lucille. "Play me a tune."

Mary sat down and lifted the cover.
She drew a shaky breath and
her fingers found the keys.
They hadn't forgotten a thing.
Soon she was riding those keys,
playing a tune that rumbled
along like a freight train.

"Lord have mercy!" said Lucille.
The teacup jumped in her hand.
She went to the stairs and called up.

"Cephus! Come down here and
hear this child play."
But Cephus was already halfway
down the stairs.

Mary's music bounced right out
the windows of Lucille's house
to the ears of all the people sitting
on the front steps.
They gathered 'round to hear the
heartbeat of Mary's music,
the bittersweet ballads,
the sorrowful spirituals.
    "Play one for me, baby!" they begged.
    "Play 'Roll, Jordan, Roll'!"

Soon people were paying her to play ... as much as fifty cents!
Mary hid away all the money they gave her. She saved it for shoes.

At school, Mary's teacher, Miss Millholland, hummed marches for her.
"Can you play that for the children when it's time to go upstairs?"
So Mary did.
But sometimes she slipped a boogie beat into those marches.
The children stopped marching and
danced on the stairs.

It seemed everyone knew about the
"little piano girl"—everyone but her family.
They found out when she broke her arm.
Mamie balanced a bottle on top of a wooden box.
"Jump over it!" she dared Mary.
When Mary fell, pain shot through her arm like lightning.

In the weeks while her arm was healing, people came and knocked on her front door.

"Where's the little piano girl?" they asked.

"Can't she come to my house to play?"

Fletcher Burley, Mary's sandy-haired stepfather from Georgia, bought her a player piano. He put it in their parlor. Fletcher bought ragtime piano rolls by James P. Johnson and Jelly Roll Morton so Mary could listen to them. In his deep, mellow voice, he sang along to "My Mama Pinned a Rose on Me." Mary listened.

"Now play it back to me, sugar," he said.

She did.

She watched the piano play, too …
and her fingers found the same notes. All she had to do was hear a tune
or see it played and she would wrap her fingers around it and never let go.

Soon Mary could tease a tune out of nowhere.
Sassy sounds slipped into her playing, sounds that
surprised her. Truck drivers stopped in the street
when they heard Mary play.

Passing policemen paused. Mary bashed beauty
out of those piano keys. Her notes took wing over her
East Liberty neighborhood till Pittsburgh's millionaires
heard them in their mansions.

When Mary cut loose, people couldn't stay still.
They set to clapping, tapping, finger-snapping.
Her blue notes made people want to cry at
just how hard life can be. Her crazy chords
made people shimmy their shoulders and
shake their heads, high and happy.
"Play it, Mary!" folks called out.
"Play 'The Tiger Rag'!"
And Mary would play a deep, powerful bass
with one hand and lay a lacework of edgy
blues over the top of it with the other.
Her music rolled and slid and jumped along,
zigzagging and giant-stepping,
until it grew too big for where she was …

For almost sixty years, Mary traveled from Kansas City to Paris.
She boogied and bebopped with the best,
with all the Kings and Dukes and Earls of jazz.
And while her fingers hopscotched across the keyboard,
banishing the bad sounds …

her toes tapped time
in beautiful shoes.

Afterword

MARY LOU WILLIAMS (1910–1981) became the most famous female jazz musician of all time, composing and arranging not only for Andy Kirk but for Duke Ellington and Benny Goodman, while playing at clubs and concerts all over the world. Always generous, she also found time to help develop the talent of others, including Charlie Parker, Thelonious Monk, and Dizzy Gillespie. She mastered every style from ragtime and stride through swing and bebop . . . and made every piece she played her own. Her spirit came through in her playing when she bowed to the past, swung through the present, and looked to the future for inspiration. And long before *feminism* was even a word, Mary was breaking down barriers in the world of jazz, a world where women sang or danced but rarely played any instrument. Duke Ellington said of her, "[Mary's] music retains a standard of quality that is timeless. She is like soul on soul."

For W, the "cat's meow."—*A.I.*

For Richard Peck.—*M.M.*

For my mom and Pia and Isabel.—*G.P.*

With thanks to Peter O'Brien, S.J.—*A.I. and M.M.*

Text copyright © 2009 by Ann Ingalls and Maryann Macdonald
Illustrations copyright © 2009 by Giselle Potter

Library of Congress Cataloging-in-Publication Data
Ingalls, Ann.
The little piano girl / by Maryann Macdonald and Ann Ingalls ; illustrated by Giselle Potter.
p. cm.
Summary: A child prodigy at the piano sprinkles her music with a little jazz.
Based on the life of the famous twentieth-century jazz musician, Mary Lou Williams.
ISBN 978-0-618-95974-7
1. Williams, Mary Lou, 1910-1981—Childhood and youth—Juvenile fiction. [1. Williams, Mary Lou, 1910-1981—Childhood and youth—Fiction.
2. Musicians—Fiction. 3. Piano—Fiction. 4. Jazz—Fiction. 5. African Americans—Fiction.] I. Ingalls, Ann. II. Potter, Giselle, ill. III. Title.
PZ7.M1486Ll 2009
[E]—dc22
2008040457

Printed in Singapore TWP 10 9 8 7 6 5 4 3 2 1